THE PEACEABLE KINGDOM IN HARTSDALE

America's First Pet Cemetery

By

EDWARD C. MARTIN, III

The Peaceable Kingdom in Hartsdale
Edward C. Martin, III
Copyright © 2013 by Edward C. Martin, III

ISBN 13: 978-1484923528
ISBN 10: 1484923529

For all information, contact:
Hartsdale Pet Cemetery & Crematory
Telephone: (914)-949-2583 or Toll Free: (800) 375-5234
Fax: (914) 949-2872
E-mail: info@petcem.com
Website: www.petcem.com

Hartsdale Pet Cemetery
75 North Central Park Avenue
Hartsdale, New York 10530

He came into my life
For want of a meal and a place to stay...
He left with my heart
— Monument inscription in
Hartsdale Pet Cemetery

Foreword

Following the initial publication of this book, Hartsdale Pet Cemetery was listed in the U.S. Department of the Interior's Registry of Historic Places. We received the great news in 2012, and it is one of the biggest milestones in our history. To give you an idea of the significance of this distinction, there are 88,000 listed properties, of which 2,698 are human cemeteries—and Hartsdale is the first and only pet cemetery to be recognized.

"I never thought more than the man on the moon that this place would grow like it has," said Dr. Samuel Johnson in 1936 shortly before his death as he gazed over thousands of monuments for beloved animals. Certainly he could not have foreseen how his little hillside orchard would become known throughout the world, or that his cemetery would now be an acknowledged place of cultural value.

While the Registry listing provides a degree of protection, it also elevates our responsibility to ensure that these historic grounds are preserved for future generations to appreciate. We look forward to the challenges and exciting future that lie ahead. We hope you will join us as we work to ensure Hartsdale continues to be a beacon for more generations of animal lovers, who, like us, will spread the word of this extraordinary place we all love so much.

– Edward C. Martin, III.
April, 2013

Contents

Acknowledgments   7

Preface   9

Introduction   11

1. Dr. Johnson's Apple Orchard 1896-1914   13

2. The Early Years 1914-1941   26

3. A Time for Change 1941-Present   41

4. The War Dog Memorial   58

5. The Peaceable Kingdom in Hartsdale   75

6. Epilogue: A Place of Peace, Beauty and Love   102

Acknowledgments

This book would not have been possible without the help of several noteworthy individuals, who I would like to thank here:

Bruce Fabricant, the director of public relations for Hartsdale, author, and close personal friend (not to mention baseball teammate) of my father. His experience, knowledge, talent and encouragement were essential in helping me publish this book.

Mary Thurston, Hartsdale's official historian, anthropologist, author, photographer and dear friend who lives in Austin, Texas. Her edits and attention to detail along with her beautiful photography and painstaking restoration of the cemetery's vast archive of photographs were invaluable. Her contagious enthusiasm and encouragement, combined with her southern charm, helped make my job much easier.

The late Malcolm Kriger, a plot-holder who in 1983 authored the first book about the cemetery, *The Peaceable Kingdom in Hartsdale*, which is the inspiration for this revised edition.

Hartsdale's founder, Dr. Samuel K. Johnson, whose compassion and vision made all of this possible. Also, all of those who followed Dr. Johnson through their leadership or contributions to the cemetery through the years, including Christian Sheu, George and Irene Lassen, Andrew Samar, Patrick and Francis Grosso.

Hartsdale's staff for their encouragement and support, including my uncle, Leonard Saccardo, cemetery foreman, Trevor Gill, my brother, Brian Martin and my sister-in-law, Saskia Martin.

The loyal, hard-working maintenance staff who keep

Hartsdale's grounds looking beautiful, including Erasmo Bautista-Velazquez, Doreteo Lino and Rene Arias.

Hartsdale's canine mascots, Susie, Brandy and Nellie.

My beloved late grandparents, Edward and Bertha Martin, who encouraged and inspired me to see just how special the Peaceable Kingdom really is.

My father, Edward C. Martin, Jr., who has taught me everything I know about life, business and sports; and my mother, Virginia Martin, who is the kindest, most loving and supportive person I know.

And my wife and best friend, Candace, our two daughters, Lilly and Charlotte, and our rescued spaniel-mix, Violet, all of whom bring so much joy to my life.

Edward C. Martin, III
Hartsdale, New York
April 2010

Preface

The year was 1980 and school had just let out for summer vacation, but I was up early getting dressed for my first day of work. Like any typical fourteen-year-old boy my head was spinning with questions, but my curiosity that morning was especially piqued by what this pet cemetery in Hartsdale was all about.

As would become the custom, I carpooled with my grandparents, Edward and Bertha Martin. My grandmother worked in the cemetery's administrative office and my grandfather was a proprietor of a well-established monument business a few miles down the road. Being the first to arrive, we were responsible for opening the gates. As we entered the historic grounds, I was immediately struck by what I saw – an emerald, dew-speckled lawn and begonias resplendent in color, with their perfume already drawing a stream of butterflies and bees. Bird calls, too many to count, echoed through the cool canopy of fir and maple trees. Squirrels, chipmunks and rabbits darted among the graves. The cemetery was coming awake in the warmth of the morning light. Its tranquil beauty was overwhelming to behold. Any preconceived ideas I had about cemeteries being gloomy places of death were immediately dispelled. This is a place that vibrates with life!

My thoughtful grandmother always brought homemade iced tea for me. Armed with sustenance, a warm smile, and well wishes, I reported for duty to Fran Grosso, the operations manager. I was assigned to my Uncle Chester (my grandmother's brother), who worked on the maintenance staff and quickly took me under his wing. A cigar-smoking prankster, I became a favorite target for many of his lighthearted jokes.

I spent the summer cutting grass, planting flowers, weeding, and running a lot of errands. In time, my brothers, Dan and Brian would join me.

In March 1982, my childhood pet died. She was a kind and gentle cocker spaniel named "Ophie." It was one of my earliest experiences with death and it had a profound effect on me. Shortly after we buried her at Hartsdale, I came to realize that my despair at Ophie's death could never diminish the joys of her life or the happiness she had brought into ours. The countless hours I had spent puzzling over the loving tributes inscribed on monuments as I went about cutting the grass now made sense to me. Having already discovered the physical beauty of the cemetery on my first day of work, I now had discovered the spiritual beauty of the Peaceable Kingdom.

It has been nearly thirty years since that fateful first day of work. After spending a few summers on the maintenance staff I moved inside to the administrative office and learned under the stewardship of my father and grandmother. After graduating from college and law school I continually found myself drawn to the Peaceable Kingdom. All of my grandparents are now resting here as are other family pets, making my connection even deeper. Sensing this passion, my father eventually offered a full-time position to me which I immediately accepted. I am very grateful that I am able to play a small part of something that is so historical, beautiful, spiritual and special.

Edward C. Martin, III

Introduction

The Peaceable Kingdom is the title of a painting by early nineteenth-century primitive painter Edward Hicks, which today hangs in the Metropolitan Museum of Art in New York City. Hicks based his work on Isaiah XI in the Bible, specifically the Noah's Ark passage, which speaks of such animals as the "wolf, lamb, leopard, lion, kid, calf...sharing the green grass where they lay." He devoted his entire artistic life to the idea of such a "Peaceable Kingdom," ultimately painting sixty-one different versions of it. But in all his canvas interpretations he showed us one thing–a world filled with love, peace and salvation, where all would be united in acceptance and understanding.

Hicks' painting is the inspiration for a 1983 book by the same title, *The Peaceable Kingdom in Hartsdale*, by the late Malcolm D. Kriger, who was a plot-holder here at the cemetery. It was the first published work to relate the story of Hartsdale, and in it Kriger chronicled dozens of heartwarming stories about the pets and people who had come here through the years. Because of the book, many began referring to the cemetery itself as the "Peaceable Kingdom," and to our delight the alternate moniker has continued to this day. So it only seems appropriate to use it again for this latest work, which will be the third book to chronicle the life of this remarkable resting place for pets.

The Peaceable Kingdom in Hartsdale not only tells of how our pet cemetery came to be, but relates stories of some of the 100,000 pets and the people who have come here since its founding in 1896. Some are famous for their work in the world of theater, literature and sports, or as financial titans and patrons of charities and the arts, and many more are everyday working people possessed of an equally exemplary devotion to their pets. Regardless of social station, they all demonstrate exceptional empathy, for they know how it feels to have loved and lost an animal companion. Then as now, they come here—to the Peaceable Kingdom—seeking a means to honor the memory of their beloved pets.

The cemetery today enjoys both national and worldwide recognition as the premier pet burial ground in America, if not the world. It is listed along with the Taj Mahal in India and Egypt's Great Pyramids of Giza as one of the top ten cemeteries in the world by the guidebook publisher Lonely Planet, which gave Hartsdale Pet Cemetery the distinction in its *Best in Travel 2009.*

And to think it all started with a spontaneous act of kindness by New York City veterinarian Dr. Samuel Johnson, who so empathized with a distraught pet owner that he suggested she bury her dog in his apple orchard. Unfortunately that woman's name is lost to the mists of time, and no stone remains to mark the fateful spot, but she can be assured that her pet is still resting peacefully within the Peaceable Kingdom of Hartsdale. Indeed, a casual stroll through the cemetery is nothing short of a trip back in time, as one can find monuments in all shapes and sizes, from the humblest to the grandest, all of them bearing messages that are poignant, inspiring or whimsical. One can also see installations that are historical precedents, such as the famous War Dog Memorial, which was the first of its kind to acknowledge the heroic service of dogs in World War I.

Regardless of tone or style, the messages left by a century of Hartsdale plot-holders contain a common thread, one which binds us not only to the past but to each other in the present–the love for an animal–so simple, so pure, so rare and so cherished.

This is the legacy of Hartsdale Pet Cemetery.

1. Dr. Johnson's Apple Orchard 1896-1913

Hartsdale Pet Cemetery began as a spin-off from a growing public health movement in the United States in the late 1800s, in which the city of New York banned the burial of animals within its limits. It was a draconian measure, leaving pet owners with few choices for a dignified interment when their animal friends died. The person who changed everything was Samuel K. Johnson. As fortune would have it, he owned a small apple orchard that stood on rough, hilly ground just twenty-five miles north from the City in the bucolic hamlet of Hartsdale in Westchester County.

Dr. Johnson had a long and distinguished career in the field of veterinary medicine, having not only served as a Professor of Veterinary Surgery at the New York Animal Hospital, but also as the official veterinarian for the State of New York. Moreover, he was a pioneer in the field of animal welfare and sat on the Board of Directors for the American Society for the Prevention of Cruelty to Animals (ASPCA) during its formative years. Yet none of this is what he is remembered for today.

In 1896, a client called on Johnson at his Manhattan office with an urgent problem. The distraught woman tearfully related how her beloved dog had just died, and that she could not bear the thought of disposing of it in the usual manner of the day. Moreover, it was illegal to bury animals in human cemeteries or in public parks. Sympathetic to her plight, the veterinarian offered to inter her pet at his orchard in Hartsdale. The woman gratefully accepted, and she made the journey to the little hamlet in Westchester.

This singular burial was not intended to be the beginning of a pet cemetery, but a short time later Dr. Johnson unwittingly gave impetus to the idea when he had lunch with a reporter friend. In the course of their casual conversation, Johnson related the story of the woman's plight and the subsequent burial of her dog. The next thing he knew, his story had appeared in print, and to his further surprise, he found himself fielding requests from others seeking a secure place to bury their beloved pets.

Soon afterward, Johnson set aside a three-acre section of the orchard, where upon the hillside quickly became dotted with markers and flower arrangements. Requests for burials continued, prompting him to implement a procedure whereby deceased pets were brought to his clinic on Twenty-Fifth Street in Manhattan in order to be documented, placed in a zinc-lined casket, and then transported to the cemetery by train. Pet owners followed up separately, often by horse-drawn carriage, to attend the burial. At the time, an interment cost ten to twenty-five dollars for a dog, and twelve dollars for a cat or other small animal. In these days that was no small amount of money, but those who loved their animals had no qualms about paying if it meant providing a secure resting place for their four-footed friends.

Word of pet burials in the little orchard spread even further after a second feature was published in the *New York Times* in 1905. As it reported, the new "canine cemetery" was in fact open to all pets, and as a result the number of burials at Hartsdale continued to grow. In these early days, individual plot-holders took personal care of their pets' graves, and the hillside became adorned with monuments, sculptures, and wrought-iron fence work as fancy as any found in human cemeteries of the day.

A rural, dirt-paved Central Park Avenue on a lazy summer afternoon in the late 1800s, just prior to the genesis of Hartsdale Pet Cemetery (located on the left).

The main entrance to the cemetery was originally located on Old Road, today known as North Washington Avenue. Early plot-holders arrived by horse-drawn carriage through this gate flanked by two tall stone pillars and the now-famous wrought iron sign bearing the cemetery's name and date of establishment. Today the iron sign can be seen at the Central Park Avenue entrance, while the stone pillars along Washington Avenue have been integrated into the fence line that encircles the grounds.

They came by carriage, which had drawn, black curtains. It was a wet, gusty April afternoon, and little eddies of vapor glistened now and again. Four men filed from the carriage and huddled toward its rear, collars up, coats buttoned tight against the swirling dampness. They shouldered a small, wreath-covered casket and slowly marched into the cemetery. Two women walked behind carrying flowers weeping silently. They were burying their dog. There was no officiating clergyman; no services at the grave. The whole ceremony lasted only about five minutes, and yet it was a remarkably fine funeral.

— New York Times, 1905

An early photo of the cemetery's east gate entrance at Central Park Avenue before the famous wrought iron sign bearing the name and establishment date of the cemetery was installed.

Besides his practice, Dr. Johnson was a Professor of Veterinary Surgery at New York University, and served as the first official veterinarian of the State of New York. He also was a pioneer in the field of animal welfare and served on the board of the ASPCA in its early years. Here Dr. Johnson is pictured with his wife, Mary, in front of the caretaker's cottage (what is now the administrative office for Hartsdale Pet Cemetery).

This simple but quaint cottage served as Dr. Johnson's summer retreat where he enjoyed peace and solace from the fast-paced climate of New York City. Today the house serves as the administrative office for Hartsdale Crematory.

This rare photograph is believed to show the site of the first burial at Hartsdale, which occurred in 1896 when Dr. Johnson kindly offered a spot to a bereaved woman seeking a safe place to bury her dog. Little did Johnson realize when he later related the tale to a reporter friend that this would mark the beginning of America's first pet cemetery. After news of the burial was printed in the *New York Times*, Johnson began receiving requests from other distraught pet owners, prompting him to set aside a three-acre section of the orchard expressly for that purpose.

By 1905 the number of burials at Hartsdale had grown to three hundred. Soon afterward the wooden picket fences were moved further down the hillside to make room for the orchard's metamorphosis into a full-scale cemetery.

By this time, a procedure had been arranged whereby each pet to be buried was brought to Dr. Johnson's New York office on Twenty-Fifth Street. The deceased animal was documented, placed in a zinc-lined casket, which was then soldered shut, and put on a train bound for Hartsdale. Pictured here is the Hartsdale train station at the turn of the century, where the caskets were received and transported to the cemetery.

Little rough mounds of earth indicate the locations of graves in the emerging pet cemetery. The earliest grave markers were simple slabs of wood bearing the number on the coffin. Soon these wooden markers would be replaced with inscribed gravestones.

Temporary wooden markers quickly gave way to elaborately engraved headstones, many of them expressing a "sincere affection for animals," according to the 1905 *New York Times* article. Hartsdale soon rivaled the finest human cemeteries of this period, with ornate iron fencework around individual plots and trellises for climbing roses.

In its formative years Hartsdale mimicked the style of fashionable Victorian human cemeteries, particularly with regard to the use of ornamental iron fencework around individual graves.

One of the most elaborate plots in Hartsdale from the turn of the century was this showpiece for a cat named "Mignon." The *New York Times* article in 1905 described it as the "largest and handsomest lot in the cemetery." Apparently, Mignon was valued at $300 in life, but much more money than that was spent after his death because a private caretaker from Woodlawn Cemetery in the Bronx was paid to keep the plot in perfect condition. This early photograph shows it adorned with two small-boxed shrubs. Flowers ring the grave, which is kept meticulously clean. The granite monument stands two and one-half feet high and features ivy leaves carved in relief along the top edge. Its inscription reads, "Mignon, Dearest and Best Beloved Friend of Ada Van Tassel Billington. Died Sept. 27, 1900."

Dr. Johnson died in 1937 and is at rest in a private family mausoleum at Woodlawn Cemetery in the Bronx, New York, not far from several of his most notable clients who buried pets at Hartsdale, among them dancer Irene Castle and Princess Vilma Lwoff-Parlaghy. Below, Hartsdale Pet Cemetery Director Edward Caterson Martin, Jr. (left) and Vice President Edward Caterson Martin, III (right) stand in front of Johnson's mausoleum.

2. The Early Years 1914–1941

In its first years of existence, Hartsdale Pet Cemetery was operated on a rather informal basis. At this point, there were no guarantees that it would exist in the long term, and whatever attention each grave received depended solely upon the individual owner. As plot-holders died, moved away or simply lost interest, some of the graves became neglected and overgrown, lending an aura of dilapidation to the grounds.

However, many wished to see the new cemetery survive. In an effort to save Hartsdale from failure, a group of plot-holders held a meeting with Dr. Johnson, during which they elected two lawyers and a judge, and drafted basic regulations for running the cemetery on a more uniform and orderly basis. On May 14, 1914, the committee officially formed a corporation and drafted by-laws. Shortly thereafter, trust funds were established and deed restrictions were filed to ensure Hartsdale's continuation in the coming decades. The property was now secure as a resting-place for the one thousand pets already interred there, with many more to come in the years ahead.

Its future ensured, the former apple orchard resumed its transformation to a manicured cemetery landscape. Additional land tracts were acquired for burials, the old wooden picket fence was replaced with one made of iron, new walkways were created, and scores of trees planted. A cottage was built for the cemetery's first full-time caretaker, while new administrative offices opened in New York City on West 45th Street. Despite World War I raging overseas, more pets were buried at Hartsdale in the three years following incorporation than in the previous twenty. By 1917, the number of graves had doubled to two thousand, and on any warm Sunday afternoon, the grounds virtually hummed with a hundred or more visitors.

Wartime belt-tightening was soon replaced with a new era of prosperity in the "Roaring Twenties," with Hartsdale hosting an increasing number of expensive and elaborate funeral and memorial arrangements for pets. Grave markers quarried from the finest granite and marble were commissioned for many pets, and affluent plot-holders paid up to four thousand dollars for interments. Among the more notable installations at the cemetery in those days of plenty was the Walsh Mausoleum. Weighing in excess of fifty tons, it is believed to be the first above-ground mausoleum ever built expressly for animals. The plot-holder, Mrs. Mary F. Walsh, exhibited extraordinary commitment to the project and supervised every detail of its construction. Also during this time, Hartsdale oversaw the installation of a grand memorial paying tribute to the dogs who served in the "war to end all wars" which is discussed in more detail in Chapter Four.

As the cemetery continued its improvements, pet-lovers from all over the world made the pilgrimage to inter their four-footed friends here, including many notable celebrities of the day. Some of these plot-holders were unconventional or far-thinking for their time, such as the flamboyant Princess Lwoff-Parlaghy, whose beloved lion cub Goldfleck rests near the cemetery office. There also is Irene Castle, the famed "flapper" dancer of the 1920s and founder of the Chicago animal shelter Orphans of the Storm who enjoyed the companionship of a little monkey named Rastas, as well as other, more conventional pets. Sandy, the devoted spaniel of Broadway actress Christine Norman, also is interred in Hartsdale. Prior to her death, the actress stipulated in her will that funds be allocated for the perpetual care of her dog's grave. Failing to appreciate the depth of her attachment to Sandy, Norman's heirs challenged her will. Ultimately though, the court ruled in her favor, setting an early legal precedent for the rights of pet owners that exists to this day.

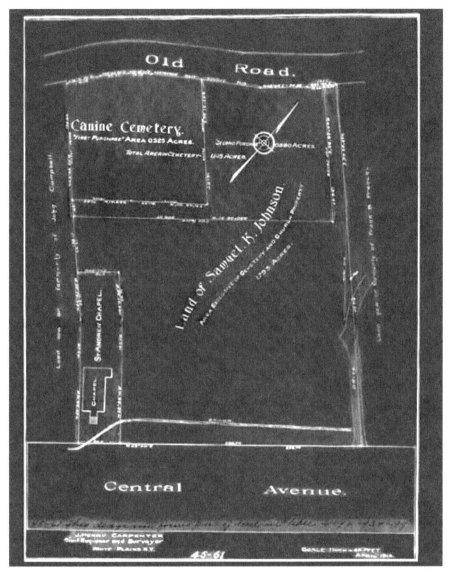

On May 14, 1914, a committee of concerned plot-holders established a corporation with formal by-laws to oversee Hartsdale. This was a key first step in maintaining the cemetery and ensuring its long-term survival.

Dog Cemetery   Hartsdale, N. Y

The land formerly known as Dr. Johnson's apple orchard underwent a rapid transformation into the manicured resting-place for pets now known as the Peaceable Kingdom. Additional tracts of land were acquired and an iron fence was erected around the perimeter, new footpaths were installed and scores of trees were planted.

A full-time caretaker was hired and a cottage for his living quarters was built. Trust funds were established to ensure the continuation of the cemetery.

Many graves became quite elaborate once the safeguards of incorporation, deed restriction and trust funds for perpetual care were implemented in the early 1900s. The land now was ensured as a resting-place for animals into the future and gave plot-holders the assurance they needed to commission highly crafted, costly memorials such as these shown.

> *Near this spot lie the remains of one who possessed beauty without vanity, strength without insolence, courage without ferocity, and all the virtues of man without his vices. This praise, which would be unmeaning flattery if inscribed over human ashes, is but a just tribute to the memory of my loving Boatswain – a dog.*
>
> —Lord Byron's *Epitaph to a Faithful Companion*, Nov. 18, 1808

The Walsh Mausoleum is located in the northwest corner of the cemetery. Weighing fifty tons, it is the largest monument ever created at Hartsdale Pet Cemetery, and is believed to be the first above-ground mausoleum ever constructed expressly for animals. Built in 1924 at a cost of $25,000, it holds the pets of Mrs. Mary F. Walsh, the wife of a wealthy real estate investor. She arrived by limousine every morning at seven o'clock to oversee its construction, and remained well after the workmen left each night. Made from the finest Vermont Barre granite, the names of two dogs, Sally and Toodles, are inscribed on the outside, along with the epitaph, "My Dear Little True-Love Hearts, Who Would Lick The Hand That Had No Food To Offer."

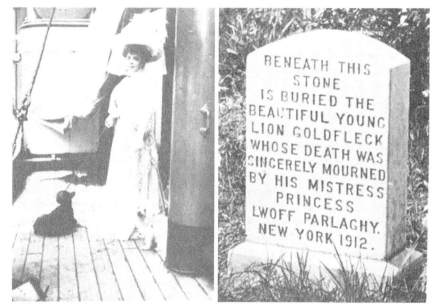

Perhaps the most unlikely pet ever buried at the cemetery is a lion cub, who was memorialized by this simple marble monument. A favorite among visitors, it reads, "Beneath this stone is buried the beautiful young lion Goldfleck, whose death is sincerely mourned by his mistress Princess Lwoff-Parlaghy." The princess, pictured here, was a well-known wealthy Hungarian artist. She was also an animal lover who raised money for some of the newly formed animal protection societies of the time. Legend has it that when she arrived in the United States in 1908, she was accompanied by a veritable menagerie of pets, including a bear, alligator, ibis, two falcons, two pet dogs and two Angora cats. Upon a visit to Ringling Brothers Circus, she fell in love with a young lion cub that she brought home by limousine to live with her and her many animal friends at the Plaza Hotel. Sadly, as the cub was growing into a full-size lion he grew ill and died. After a formal wake at the Plaza, the princess took Goldfleck to Hartsdale for burial in 1912.

Among the international celebrities who came to the cemetery in the 1920s, Irene Castle is distinctive for her humanitarian accomplishments. Although Irene and her husband, Vernon, were wildly popular as trendsetters in dance and fashion, she preferred to be known as a champion of humane causes, having founded the still-active Orphans of the Storm animal shelter near Chicago in 1928. One of her dogs at Hartsdale, Zowie, was depicted in the 1939 Ginger Rogers-Fred Astaire movie, *The Story of Irene and Vernon Castle*. She is pictured here with her pet monkey, "Rastas," who she called "the smartest most lovable monkey that ever lived."

A Broadway actress once declared one of the twelve most beautiful women in the world, Christine Norman had a far-reaching effect on pet burials in America. A few years after she interred her dog, Sandy, in Hartsdale, Norman leaped to her death from the twentieth story of a New York City hotel. It was major news, made all the more sensational by revelations that her will included directions for money to go to the upkeep of her pet's grave. Christine's mother contested the will in court, claiming that her daughter was "obviously of unsound mind and the victim of fraud and undue influence," but the attorney representing the estate maintained that Norman's last request "reflected the thoughts and concerns of a caring, loving woman of integrity." The court agreed, ruling the will valid and setting a legal precedent that has to this day protected the wishes of other pet lovers in similar situations. This rare illustration shows Christine Norman with Sandy, her beloved Japanese Spaniel, in the 1920s hit *Peg O' My Heart*.

Ninety years of celebrities have passed through the gates of the Peaceable Kingdom to lay their pets to rest, and while some of their names may be unfamiliar to this generation, they were as prominent as any movie star today. Early television personality Kate Smith brought her dog Freckles to Hartsdale in 1953, as did world famous bandleader Gene Krupa, who interred his two dogs, Jerk and Susie. Others from the world of stage, motion pictures, radio and television include Barbara Bennett, Dagmar, Barry Gray, Edwin C. Hill, Evelyn Nesbitt, and George Raft. Also we see the names of singer Robert Merrill, sports figures Ralph Kiner, Joe Garagiola and Allie Sherman and the infamous millionaire Hetty Green – whose dog was aptly named Money.

While sightings of the famed and fortuned in Hartsdale are not as common today, some of the more contemporary celebrities who have come to the Peaceable Kingdom include singer Mariah Carey, music executive Tommy Mottola, music producer Phil Ramone, celebrity chef Rocco DiSpirito and television personality Stephen Glover (A.K.A., "Steve-O"). Pictured here is Mariah Carey's memorial for her cat, Clarence, which is signed "Love, M."

Some pets themselves were famous, such as the eight champion Irish Setters buried in the distinguished Cheever-Porter plot.

Other pets like "Irish" spent much of their lives in animal shelters. So named for his breed, the Irish Setter pup was picked up during a routine roundup of strays by the Bronx SPCA, and although the shelter tried to find him a good home, he seemed determined to break free and return to the pound by his own volition. After several failed attempts to get him happily resettled, a saloonkeeper said he

would take Irish in. Although being warned about his previous escapes, the man was so confident that Irish would stay with him that he wagered one hundred dollars on it. Sure enough, the determined dog found his way back to the SPCA. This time Irish had made his point, so the SPCA relented and allowed him to stay at the shelter. The saloonkeeper paid the hundred dollars, and years later when Irish died the money was used to purchase his plot and headstone at Hartsdale.

3. A Time for Change 1941–Present

The Great Depression that rippled across the United States in the 1930s saw the abandonment and closure of countless cemeteries, but with income generated from the trusts that were wisely established shortly after the time of incorporation, Hartsdale Pet Cemetery managed to weather the storm. Dr. Johnson passed away on August 3, 1937 at the age of eighty-three, and in the wake of his death, the cemetery found itself somewhat rudderless. Ordinarily a painstakingly detailed man, Johnson – uncharacteristically, it would appear – had done nothing to plan for a successor. Thus, the job of running the cemetery fell to the executors of his estate. Hartsdale functioned under absentee management for four years, but it became clear that the time to seek new leadership had come.

In 1941, one of the estate's executors approached Christian Scheu about taking on the job. Scheu was a mechanic who owned a business nearby, and he had lived across the street from the cemetery since childhood. He frequently cut through the peaceful grounds after work and enjoyed stopping to chat with the caretaker. Seeing this as an opportunity to do something that greatly interested him, Sheu enlisted the help of his childhood friend and business partner, C. George Lassen, and on December 31, 1941, the two men assumed responsibility for the cemetery.

Significant changes followed under their stewardship as the cemetery was operated with a more "hands-on" approach. They closed the administrative office in New York in 1942, transferred all the records back to Hartsdale, and George Lassen and his wife, Irene, moved into the original vacation home of Dr. Johnson on the grounds. For the first time, somebody was on the premises around the clock.

The two men, aided by their families' hard work and dedication, erased the effects of years of neglect. The fruits of their labor began to show, as the beauty of the cemetery not only was restored but surpassed the glorious 1920s. As in earlier years, Hartsdale continued to be a draw for many well-known personalities. Moreover, with the Great Depression a thing of the past, a growing number of middle-class families were bringing their animal friends to the Peaceable Kingdom.

George Lassen died in 1961 and Christian Scheu retired soon after, leaving the job of operating the cemetery to George Lassen's widow, Irene, and her son, Ray, who continued on another twelve years. By 1973, Mrs. Lassen had spent thirty years of her life in the former apple orchard, and understandably, her feelings for the Peaceable Kingdom ran very deep. She wanted to be sure that her successor not only shared her love of this sacred place, but also was astute in business matters as the changing times demanded.

One day Mrs. Lassen mentioned her plans for retirement to monument designer and plot-holder Edward Caterson Martin, Sr., whom she had come to respect and admire. A master craftsman of some of the cemetery's most beautiful monuments, Martin suggested she consult with his son, Ed Jr., who at the time worked as a certified public accountant. What started out as a simple meeting to provide "a little tax advice" turned into a life-changing offer to run America's first pet cemetery. Just as Christian Scheu had done thirty-five years before, Edward Martin enlisted the help of his long-time friend, Patrick Grosso, and on April 17, 1974, the young men officially took the helm at Hartsdale. Together, they utilized the same business paradigm that had been used with such success by Scheu and Lassen – a hands-on, family-operated approach to the business. Martin enlisted the help of his mother, Bertha, his brother-in-law, Len Saccardo and his uncle, Chester Reynolds, while Grosso brought his brother, Fran, on board. In the years to come, other relatives would join the Harstdale team, along with their children.

Four decades later, Hartsdale Pet Cemetery has remained at the forefront of the pet after-care industry, and today it is recognized as one of the most successful and beautifully maintained animal burial grounds not only in America but in the world. In 2009 it was listed as one of the top-ten resting places by Lonely Planet, a publisher of travel guidebooks, putting it in the company of the Taj Mahal and the Great Pyramids of Giza. Most recently, in recognition of the unique history that has transpired here, Hartsdale has been recognized by the U.S. Department of the Interior as a place of national historic significance, giving rise to a new and expanded directive to preserve the many monuments and natural features that have made the Peaceable Kingdom uniquely relevant to animal lovers in this new century.

Following the death of Dr. Johnson, Christian Scheu became the co-Director of Hartsdale Pet Cemetery with his friend and business associate C. George Lassen. He lived across the street from the cemetery most of his life, and could recall the grounds as they looked in the early years, when horses pulled wagons up Central Park Avenue on the final leg of their journey from Johnson's office in the City. He retired in 1963 but continued to visit the Peaceable Kingdom well into his late nineties.

George Lassen moved his family into Dr. Johnson's former summer home on the cemetery grounds, marking the first time somebody was on the premises night and day. He is pictured here playing with Hartsdale's first official mascot, Susie, who was adopted by the Lassens in April 1945.

"One of my most poignant memories was of a couple who often visited the cemetery during the Korean War. They had suffered a shattering loss. Their son had been killed when he stepped on a land mine while on patrol. He was buried in an unknown grave in that far-off foreign land. A short time after the young man was killed, his childhood dog also died and was brought to Hartsdale. The man and wife came every week with flowers. They thought of the spot where the dog was buried as a place where they could feel closer to their son."

— Irene Lassen

Irene Lassen managed the cemetery with dignity and excellence until her retirement in 1974. She is pictured here with her son, Ray who joined the family business after graduating from college in 1958. Mother and son are posed at the grave of Jack (James) McPherson, the Mystery Chef of radio fame, whose cremains along with those of his wife are in a bronze urn anchored to the stone above the grave of their dogs.

Following the harsh days of the Depression, the hard work of George Lassen and Chris Scheu restored the cemetery to splendor and grace.

Edward Caterson Martin, Sr., a master stone engraver, followed in the footsteps of his cousin, Robert Caterson, who designed the War Dog Memorial at Hartsdale. For more than forty years, Martin, Sr. created magnificent monuments from his nearby studio, turning America's first pet cemetery into a showcase of ultimate artistic expression.

Bertha Martin, the wife of Edward C. Martin, Sr. and mother of current Director Edward C. Martin, Jr., worked in Hartsdale's office for more than twenty years. To this day, plot-holders remember her compassion, sensitivity and kindness.

Edward C. Martin, Jr. has been the Director of Hartsdale since 1974, but his family's ties to the cemetery go back five generations. Not only under his watch has the ground's historic beauty been protected, but he's worked diligently to provide the cemetery with a secure future for yet another century.

Pat Grosso was the co-Director of Hartsdale Pet Cemetery from 1974 until his retirement in 1997.

Fran Grosso is pictured with his dog, Brandy, a former stray, who was Hartsdale's second canine mascot. Fran, who is Pat's brother, was the cemetery's operations manager before moving to his current position at Hartsdale Crematory.

What began as a business venture would soon become a personal passion for Hartsdale Director Ed Martin, Jr., pictured here in the spring of 2009 with his wife Ginny. After thirty years of service, Martin sees a common thread linking the rich and the poor, the mighty and the meek – the simple love of a pet.

The Martin family affiliation with Hartsdale continues in the 21st century with Ed Martin, Jr's sons, Ed, III (top) and Brian (bottom, with his dog Nellie, Hartsdale's current mascot), playing an integral role in continuing the cemetery's tradition of excellence.

Ed Martin Jr.'s brother-in-law, Len Saccardo, has been the cemetery's administrator since 1975.

Hartsdale foreman Trevor Gill has been keeping the grounds at the Peaceable Kingdom beautiful since 1976.

Hartsdale Pet Cemetery's 100th anniversary in 1996 was a cause for celebration. Apple trees were replanted on the grounds as a symbolic nod to the cemetery's orchard origins, and on September 29th a special get-together marking the centennial drew hundreds of plot-holders and well wishers, along with dignitaries from local and county governments. Also in attendance was former cemetery Director Irene Lassen and Eva Scheu, the widow of Christian Scheu. The highlight of the festivities was the unveiling of the three-piece Centennial Memorial. Its centerpiece bears a bronze plaque telling the story of that fateful day in 1896, when Dr. Johnson kindly opened his private summer retreat to a pet owner in need. Flanking the monument are two six-foot obelisks honoring those who have served or contributed to the cemetery in the decades that followed, starting with the Lassen, Scheu, Martin and Grosso families. The names of benefactors and patrons of the cemetery's beautification program have continued to be added since its dedication.

53

The cemetery is always evolving to keep up with the times. In 1986 a state-of-the art crematory was installed on the grounds to address the growing demand for a dignified alternative to traditional burials and a special section has been established for the interment of cremains, along with a dedicated Memorial Garden for those preferring to scatter their pets' ashes.

In addition to its significance as a historic site, Hartsdale is a Certified Wildlife Habitat and abounds with native fauna common in this once-rural valley a hundred years ago.

In recent decades, Hartsdale has further expanded to include several new sections for pet burial.

In 2005, plot-holder Tony LaMura built an above-ground mausoleum for his dog, Sandy. It is a smaller replica of Mr. LaMura's family mausoleum at Woodlawn Cemetery in the Bronx, and only the second such structure to be built at Hartsdale since the Walsh Mausoleum in 1924. Weighing in excess of five tons, Sandy's house of rest sits on a concrete foundation that is seven feet deep and reinforced with 1,500 pounds of stainless steel marine-grade rebar. The exterior is made of the finest Barre Vermont granite and the ornate bronze door is inlaid with copper. The interior is finished in highly polished granite and contains an inscription in gold leaf lettering.

The year 2012 saw the listing of Hartsdale Pet Cemetery on the U.S. Department of the Interior's National Registry of Historic Places. The unveiling of a dedicational plaque recognizing the Registry listing was attended by local dignitaries and the President of the International Association of Pet Cemeteries and Crematories.

Left, Hartsdale Pet Cemetery is the first animal burial ground in America to keep a Historian on its staff. Anthropologist and animal scholar Mary Thurston has been working with the cemetery since 1996.

DEDICATED
TO THE MEMORY OF
THE WAR DOG
ERECTED BY PUBLIC CONTRIBUTION
BY DOG-LOVERS, TO MAN'S MOST
FAITHFUL FRIEND, FOR THE VALIANT
SERVICES RENDERED IN THE
WORLD WAR
1914 — 1918

4. The War Dog Memorial

When you first step through the cemetery gate on Central Park Avenue, your eyes are immediately pulled upward toward the summit where an American flag flies. Underneath it he stands, a noble German shepherd of bronze. The inscription on the stone at his feet calls him a "War Dog," and while he might not be instantly familiar to passersby today, he once was hailed the world over as a hero of limitless and unconditional courage.

In anticipation of World War I in 1914, the Allied Forces conscripted thousands of dogs, and for the first time, many were specifically trained to seek out critically wounded soldiers. Deployed by the international Red Cross, these predecessors to today's search-and-rescue canines were undeterred by whizzing bullets or exploding artillery as they canvassed pocked battlefield landscapes for lost soldiers who were too hurt to call for help on their own. Time and again, the fearless dogs saved America's fathers and sons so they might return home, and as stories of their valor made headlines here in the States, the pet-loving public overwhelmingly came to see these animals as heroes in their own right. Not surprisingly, when the idea was broached about creating a memorial tribute to the dogs of this Great War, it was embraced with enthusiasm.

Proponents suggested that the pet cemetery in Hartsdale was the perfect setting for this special homage. One particular high-spot along the ridge overlooking busy Central Park Avenue below seemed ideal, and Johnson was happy to donate the chosen parcel toward this end. Estimates for the memorial topped $2,500, a sizeable amount of money at the time, so the cemetery sent out a letter calling for contributions to help defray costs. Donations poured in, both from Hartsdale's plot-holders and the public at large–even school children sent in their precious pennies for the project. A letter addressed to donors dated September 12, 1921 describes the planned installation as a "rustic boulder executed in 'Rock of Ages' Barre Vermont granite, surmounted by a heroic statue of a War Dog, canteen, and helmet in bronze." As the letter so aptly predicted, the monument would be one "which will live for ages and be a reminder to our posterity of recognition of [the War Dog's] invaluable service."

Robert Caterson, the acclaimed builder of monuments and distinguished public works such as Grand Central Terminal in New York City, was tapped to oversee the project, along with designer Walter A. Buttendorf. (Coincidentally, Caterson is a cousin of Hartsdale's current Director, Edward Caterson Martin, Jr.). Selecting a ten-ton granite boulder from his own Vermont quarry, Caterson painstakingly crafted the stone to resemble the rugged topography of a battlefield. The larger-than-life bronze dog, with the universally-recognized symbol of the Red Cross emblazoned on the blanket across his back, was reportedly modeled after a particularly striking German shepherd that was taken on its daily walk past Buttendorf's office. The War Dog stands in perpetual alert, with eyes sharply focused and his ears pricked forward, ready to leap into action at a moment's notice. The canteen and shrapnel-dented helmet at his feet really tell the story–it was the Red Cross dog who brought reviving spirits to the wounded soldier, then retrieved his helmet to alert stretcher-bearers waiting back in the trenches that somebody alive had been found.

A concise but powerful inscription graces the boulder's face: "Dedicated to the memory of the WAR DOG. Erected by public contribution by dog lovers, to man's most faithful friend for the valiant services rendered in the World War. 1914-1918."

The monument's 1923 unveiling was attended by representatives of every nation caught in this "war to end all wars." Had those onlookers been able to see into the future they may have altered the inscription, as no one at the time could envision that a second global conflict would follow, let alone that dogs would yet again stand at the sides of men on the field of battle. Even in this age of computerized electronics, dogs alone remain infallible as detectors of explosives and other possible threats to our troops. When their civilian service as assistants to the disabled and protectors of police and firemen is taken into consideration, it becomes immediately evident that humanity will continue to depend on the humble canine for years to come. Hartsdale Pet Cemetery believes all service dogs are heroes, regardless of where they apply their skills, and to that end a special ceremony held every year in June to pay them proper tribute concludes with the laying of a wreath at the base of the Red Cross dog on the summit.

The War Dog Memorial at the cemetery's summit is clearly visible from the gate on Central Park Avenue. These two pictures show the memorial from this vantage point, as it appeared around 1940 and today.

This rare photograph shows famed monument designer Robert Caterson at his 92nd birthday party (labeled above his head with the number 2). With the help of Walter Buttendorf (fourth from the right, labeled 1), Caterson created Hartsdale's famous War Dog Memorial, which was dedicated in 1923.

DEDICATED
TO THE MEMORY OF
THE WAR DOG
ERECTED BY PUBLIC CONTRIBUTION
BY DOG LOVERS. TO MAN'S MOST
FAITHFUL FRIEND. FOR THE VALIANT
SERVICES RENDERED IN THE
WORLD WAR
1914 — 1918

Using the finest granite from his own Vermont quarry, Robert Caterson fashioned this ten-ton boulder to serve as a base for the bronze rendering of a Red Cross dog from World War I. The canine hero stands ever vigilant, his eyes focused on some distant point in a battlefield from times past. The canteen and shrapnel-dented helmet at his feet symbolize his service as a savior for lost and wounded soldiers. Today the War Dog Memorial is designated as a landmark in Westchester County and is listed in the Art Inventories Catalog of the Smithsonian.

What strikes visitors are the eyes, as the dog seems to gaze beyond you, searching, looking for something or someone – a dog in the midst of his work.

Never forgotten, the hero canines of war are honored at the War Dog Memorial Celebration every year in June. The tradition began decades ago when a World War II veteran of the Battle of the Bulge known only as Arthur came to the cemetery every Memorial Day to place a wreath at base of the memorial. Hartsdale has continued the tradition at the War Dog Memorial Celebration. Hundreds of people attend the annual service, which pays tribute not only to military canines but to all manner of service dogs. Pictured here is David Nastri of the National Guard placing a wreath, with cemetery Vice President Edward C. Martin, III and Hartsdale's chaplain, the Reverend David James, looking on.

Hartsdale is the resting place to many animal war heroes, among them Scamp, a World War II canine soldier, and Joachim, who returned from the Vietnam War to live the rest of his days with a loving family. The United States deployed thousands of dogs in Europe and the Pacific during World War II, marking the beginning of a tradition that continued in Korea, Vietnam, and now the Middle East.

Robby was an aging explosives detection dog who was the inspiration behind the creation of a retirement law for military working dogs. The national "Save Robby" campaign in 2000 was a rallying point for thousands of pet-lovers who petitioned lawmakers to pass America's first federal law stipulating an adoption alternative to euthanasia for military dogs when they become injured or too old to continue the arduous work of protecting our troops. After his death, Robby's cremated remains were personally delivered to Hartsdale by Major John Probst from Lackland Air Force Base in San Antonio, Texas, where today's

war dogs are trained and paired with their human handlers. Robby's interment ceremony, which was filmed by The History Channel, took place at the War Dog Memorial Celebration in June 2001, complete with a Color Guard firing detail and bugler from the American Legion. Pictured here is Robby with his handler Lance Corporal Shawnn Manthey.

Police dog burials are conducted at Hartsdale Pet Cemetery with honors befitting of any fallen human officer.

CASEY
METRO NORTH P.D.
MY PARTNER
OUR BEST FRIEND
1983 — 1994

Remembrances for firedogs are also conducted at Hartsdale Pet Cemetery, one of the more interesting ones being for a little canine named Kerry, who became the subject of a children's book published by Rand McNally and Company in 1949. A mascot for Hook and Ladder Company Number 29 of the New York City Fire Department, Kerry gave his life in the line of duty in 1942. He was buried in Hartsdale but a proper monument was not installed at that time, something the cemetery was happy to redress during its annual War Dog Memorial service in 2007.

IN MEMORY OF THE HEROIC CANINE
SIRIUS
AND ALL THOSE WHO LOST THEIR LIVES
AS A RESULT OF THE
TERRORIST ATTACK ON
THE WORLD TRADE CENTER ON
SEPTEMBER II, 2001

Animals who are called upon to serve our needs sometimes make the supreme sacrifice. Sirius, a yellow Labrador retriever, was the only police dog to die at the World Trade Center from the terrorist attacks on September 11, 2001. His remains were found four months later and carried out of the rubble with full police honors. After cremation at Hartsdale, the dog's remains were returned to his handler, making this particular Hartsdale memorial a cenotaph, not a grave marker.

DEDICATED TO
THE CANINES AND THEIR TRAINERS
WHO SO NOBLY SERVED AS PART OF THE
FEDERAL EMERGENCY MANAGEMENT AGENCY TASK FORCE
URBAN SEARCH AND RESCUE MISSION
IN OKLAHOMA CITY IN APRIL 1995

Motivated by the heroic efforts of the canines who assisted in the search for survivors of the disastrous 1995 federal office building bombing in Oklahoma City, Hartsdale Pet Cemetery installed a memorial marker honoring those who participated in the rescue mission.

Away from the fields of battle there are pets at Hartsdale who served in other ways. These "saviors on the home front" include guide dogs who were the eyes and ears for people without sight or hearing as well as therapy dogs.

In addition to its June commemorative of service animals, Hartsdale also celebrates National Pet Memorial Day each September. The program includes a traditional blessing of the animals in which pet owners receive blessings for their animal friends both living and deceased. Cemetery chaplain, the Reverend David James, has helped conduct these events on our grounds for many years now. The blessing of the animals honors a longtime Christian tradition stemming from the days of St. Francis of Assisi, who was known as a lover of animals and nature. Pictured here is Reverend James blessing Olive the English Springer spaniel.

Each December Hartsdale Pet Cemetery holds a tree lighting ceremony to honor the memory of all animal companions. As part of the occasion, the cemetery asks for donations of pet food from plot-holders and from the general public, which is then given to local animal shelters in Westchester and Rockland counties.

The Peaceable Kingdom has long been a place where the bonds of unconditional love between humans and animals are honored and remembered, and it is now also a place where new bonds are born. Hartsdale has partnered with The Shelter Pet Alliance since 2002 to conduct adoption events at the annual War Dog and Pet Memorial Day celebrations.. These highly successful events have placed hundreds of needy dogs and cats into permanent loving homes.

5. The Peaceable Kingdom in Hartsdale

If the story of America's first pet cemetery holds any message, it certainly is that the death of an animal can be every bit as emotional an experience as the death of a person. Four footed or not, these are our dear friends, and they have been lost to us.

Even in this modern age, anguish for a departed animal seems little changed from that fateful day in 1896 when the first dog came to the apple orchard to be laid to rest. The sentiments we find inscribed on a century of gravestones here at Hartsdale resonate with a joy that knows no time, and for kinships born of trust and acceptance. More than ever, these voices from the past validate our deepest-held beliefs about the pets who share our every hardship, happiness, or sorrow.

Here, inside the Peaceable Kingdom, all are bound by this thread of love.

The Peaceable Kingdom in Hartsdale provides refuge to visiting pet owners, and a chance to reflect on times past with beloved companions. Every day many come, even years later, to express their enduring love.

Placed here just three years after Dr. Johnson's apple orchard began its transformation into America's first cemetery for pets, this stone is inscribed to "Dotty, beloved pet of E.M. Dodge, who died in her fourteenth year." It bears the date September 16, 1899, making it the oldest surviving grave marker on the grounds.

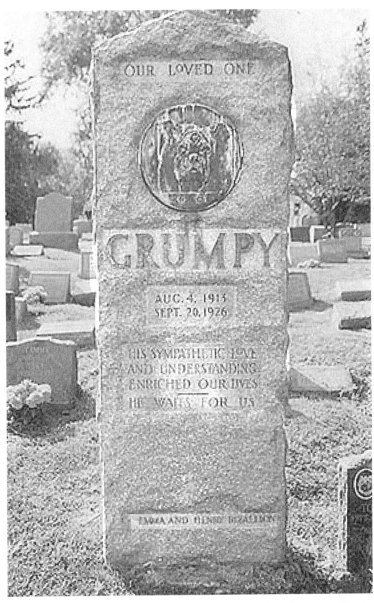

For years the tallest monument in Hartsdale was for Grumpy the bulldog, who died in 1926. It stood over six feet in height, but the foundation had weakened through the years and the stone was at risk of tipping over, leaving the cemetery no alternative but to cut the monument into two pieces. The marker has since been reset with a new foundation. Underneath the bronze relief bearing Grumpy's likeness is carved, "His sympathetic love and understanding enriched our lives. He waits for us."

One of the more unique pet tributes on the Hartsdale grounds is this French LeMans racing trophy, which graces the grave of a poodle named Black Brook Vin. A touching tribute to "Vinny Boy" recounts how the dog "clowned, played and loved people as much as any mongrel on earth." Throughout his life Vinny maintained a canine passion for his master's race-winning Bentley Marquee. "This champion's trophy is his headstone," the inscription continues, "no other person is more deserving."

The Peaceable Kingdom in Hartsdale is a veritable gallery of distinctive sculptures and statuary, from dogs and cats to angels and arches.

Throughout Hartsdale's landscape, visitors are greeted by unique sculptures such as this 1942 stone dog house for Buster and Queenie, while the exquisitely detailed cat basket rendered in marble is for felines named, Tang, Woo Tai and Yuan.

In graceful bas-relief on white marble is the 1923 stone for Silver Prince, a Persian cat.

Also carved in relief is the 1902 marker for Babe the terrier, who was a companion to George Primrose of the popular turn-of-the-century minstrel team "Primrose and West."

Thor is memorialized with a sculpture of a dog holding a basket in his mouth, and watching alongside over his grave are a pair of white doves.

The oval shaped marker (left) incorporates a line drawing by a plot-holder who is an artist. Look carefully and you will see a self-portrait of the woman embracing her beloved canine friend.

Poetry abounds at Hartsdale Pet Cemetery. The Rosen family erected this distinctive monument depicting the turning pages of a book in honor of their many pets. The inscription reads, "A Page is turned / Present to past...Still in our hearts / Because our love lasts. . ."

Mr. & Mrs. Don Oberwager's final resting place for a dog named Thor expresses the most prevalent wish of plot-holders in the Peaceable Kingdom– that of some day being reunited with their animal friends.

The myth that animals have no souls has been put to rest at Hartsdale. Religious themes abound on the markers scattered throughout the grounds, representing diverse faiths. Some incorporate images of Jesus or various saints, and in one case both the Cross and the Star of David, an ultimate expression of the Peaceable Kingdom as a place of ecumenical acceptance and freedom.

While Hartsdale is best known as a cemetery for animals, there is no prohibition against burying the cremated remains of people. To date more than seven hundred people have opted for joint-interment with their pets here, such as Peter Palumbo, who now rests with his beloved animal friends. His headstone features the Masonic Square and Compasses, symbolizing his association with the Freemasons.

Much like the 1920's dancer and humanitarian Irene Castle, Sandra Rindner was an influential force in New York's canine community. Her nonprofit organization, Miss Rumple's Orphanage, rescues rehomes miniature dogs who have been abandoned or fallen on hard times. Upon her death in 2006, Rindner left directions that her cremated remains be interred in Hartsdale with her predeceased dogs. Thirty mourners, including one state Senator, attended the graveside funeral.

Following the lead of Christine Norman, many plot-holders make provisions for the perpetual care of their pets' graves. In 1946, the will of Mrs. Cornelia Polhemus Meserole included directions for ten thousand dollars to be given to Hartsdale for the upkeep of her dogs' monument, which was installed in 1914.

A cursory search of Hartsdale records will find that almost every part of the world is represented here, beginning with the dog Roma, who was born in Rome, Italy. This is one of the earliest known foreign pets to enter the Peaceable Kingdom, having arrived in 1909.

From London, England came Mrs. Jennie Owens' black Pomeranian, "Rags," who died in 1921. Other countries represented in the cemetery include Germany, France, Holland, Scotland, Japan and Russia

Beloved Egypt, who was born in the land by the same name, probably journeyed farther in life than any other pet in Hartsdale. The inscription reads, "Beloved Egypt, who lies beneath this stone after a journey of thirty thousand miles. Weary traveler now at rest. Little Traveler God knew best."

Hartsdale's Peaceable Kingdom is a true melting pot. Born in Russia, this inscription for Charlie reads, "Love You Always. . . Mama, Papa, Sveta."

Worlds come together in many, many ways at Hartsdale.

Hartsdale Pet Cemetery is a true mixing pot, where the themes of love, companionship shine through linguistic and cultural barriers.

Ties to far away homelands are evident throughout Hartsdale. Perhaps a pet's family, continuing a tradition of their own origin, inspired them to engrave many different languages on these monuments. Chinese characters abound, as do Egyptian hieroglyphics, or international terms of affection such as, "La Buena," "Siempre," "Jolie," "Toujours," "Amico," "Estaras," "Adorad Companerito," "Zuckerpuppe" and "Mein."

Considering the many nations, religions, cultures and beliefs found at Hartsdale, this hallowed place is a veritable United Nations, where peaceful coexistence is alive and well.

Musical themes are popular at the Peaceable Kingdom and it comes as no surprise that some memorials like those for Shadow and Tristan incorporate sheet music and musical notes. Shadow's memorial has the actual notes for *Me and My Shadow*, a popular song from 1927 that was later recorded by Sammy Davis, Jr. and Ted Lewis, among others.

Another related musical theme is that of popular bands and famous concerts.

The sun, moon and stars are common astronomical themes on grave markers. Sputnik, a pet born in 1957, was named after the historic Russian space flight that took place the same year. Other markers are pets by the names of Comet, Star, Galaxy, Sunshine and Lilly, who "was not the sunshine, was not the sunset, she was the sun."

Pets with high I.Q.'s sometimes are named after civilization's greatest thinkers, such as the Greek philosophers Aristotle and Plato.

These gifted pets took their names from history's greatest playwrights, Shakespeare and Chaucer.

Pets also are celebrated for their most notable attributes, such as courage, power, beauty and strength.

The intoxicating effect of a pet's love has even motivated some to christen their companions with the names of favorite cocktails. In this regard, Hartsdale boasts a well-stocked liquor cabinet, including Whiskey, Drambuie, Brandy, Champagne, Bourbon, Vodka, Martini and Daiquiri.

In the end, though, one theme transcends all–that of loyalty and friendship. Some consider their animals to be devoted pets, while to others they are their best friend. . .

...and to a few, they are their only friend.

6. Epilogue: A Place of Peace, Beauty and Love

It has been more than one hundred years since Dr. Johnson first opened his little orchard to a grieving dog owner. Today, more than 70,000 beloved pets rest here, representing not only a diverse array of companion animals but people from all walks of life. The end result is a place of profound love and beauty.

Today, Hartsdale stands alone as the first and perhaps greatest perpetual memorial to animals everywhere. It virtually sings with love, and of growing things that pass through the cycles of the seasons, only to burst forth anew each spring. Some would even say that the cemetery itself has a soul.

Malcolm D. Kriger phrased it best in the book he authored in 1983:

Today at the cemetery, cats, snakes, dogs, hamsters, alligators, chickens, gerbils, rabbits, turtles, pigs, goldfish, mice, pigeons, guinea pigs and the lion 'Goldfleck' continue to 'live' in a world of love and peace. And with them still, are lovely trees and flowers, ageless rocks, lush grass, darting insects, and birds and small animals that visit at night. This is the way it has been, the way it is, the way it will always be.

This is the Peaceable Kingdom in Hartsdale.

Views from the west entrance of the cemetery on Washington Avenue, as it looked a century ago and today.

A westward view of the cemetery, as it looked nearly a century ago and the same view today.

This view is from one of the first burial sections of the cemetery, past and present.

Winding paths, flowering cherry trees and a babbling brook dot Hartsdale's landscape today.

From the cemetery's peak, visitors can take in the Peaceable Kingdom's breathtaking beauty.

As visitors amble along the cemetery's footpaths they can see how each monument stands as tribute to the joy a pet brought to someone's life.

William Gladstone, the Prime Minister of England under Queen Victoria, once declared, "Show me the manner in which a nation cares for its dead and I will measure with mathematical exactness the tender sympathies of its people, their respect for the law and their loyalty to high ideals." The manner with which we pay our last respects to those we love, human or animal, reflects our sense of the meaning of life, not death. That is why there were ceremonial burials for pets going on five thousand years ago, and that is why burials will continue at Hartsdale Pet Cemetery–as long as there are animal companions and people who love them, we will be here.

About The Author

EDWARD C. MARTIN, III is the Vice President of Hartsdale Pet Cemetery. Raised in Bronxville, New York, he is the eldest son of cemetery Director, Edward C. Martin, Jr. Edward III's association with Hartsdale spans thirty years, beginning as a teen when he spent his summers at the cemetery cutting grass and planting flowers. He received an undergraduate degree from Iona College, a law degree from Pace Law School, and he is a Certified Public Accountant. Following a successful career at Price Waterhouse, he returned to his roots working at the pet cemetery. Today he lives in Bronxville, with his wife, Candace, his two daughters, Lilly and Charlotte, and his pets Violet, a rescued spaniel-mix, and two guinea pigs named George and Hunny Bunny.

Made in the USA
Middletown, DE
27 March 2025

73303577R00066